How Do You S

Ellen Javernick

Rigby®

A Harcourt Achieve Imprint

www.Rigby.com
1-800-531-5015

How do you sleep?

Most people sleep in beds.
Some pets sleep in beds, too.

2

Do you sleep upside down?

Some animals sleep upside down.
Bats sleep upside down in caves.

Other animals sleep upside down, too.
Sloths sleep upside down in trees.

Do you sleep standing up?

Some animals do.
Giraffes and horses can sleep
standing up.

Do you sleep with your eyes open?

Fish and snakes keep their eyes open
all the time.
You can't tell if they are sleeping.

Do you sleep in the daytime?

Some animals do.

Owls and raccoons sleep until dark.

At night you go to bed,
but some animals are just getting up.
They go out to find things to eat at night.

Do you sleep for days and days without waking up?

Some animals sleep all winter.

First they eat a lot, and then they sleep.

They don't have to get up for a long time.

Do you sometimes sleep with your mom or dad?

Some animals sleep
with their moms and dads, too.

Some animals sleep together.

Do you need to sleep?
Do animals need to sleep?

Yes, everybody needs to sleep!

16